BUILDING
WORLD LANDMARKS

The
White House

by Joanne Mattern

BLACKBIRCH PRESS
An imprint of Thomson Gale, a part of The Thomson Corporation

THOMSON
GALE

Detroit • New York • San Francisco • San Diego • New Haven, Conn. • Waterville, Maine • London • Munich

PICTURE CREDITS:
Cover Image: © age/footstock/SuperStock
© Bettmann/CORBIS, 6, 24
© CORBIS, 4, 16, 21
© Free Agents Limited/CORBIS, 42
Getty Images, 18
Library of Congress, 8, 28, 31, 34
Maury Aaseng, 10, 32, 40
White House Historical Association, 15

LIBRARY OF CONGRESS CATALOGING-IN-PUBLICATION DATA

Mattern, Joanne, 1963–
   The White House / by Joanne Mattern.
     p. cm. — (Building world landmarks)
   Includes bibliographical references and index.
   ISBN 1-4103-0561-9 (hardcover : alk. paper)
    1. White House (Washington, D.C.)—Juvenile literature. 2. Washington (D.C.)—
Buildings, structures, etc.—Juvenile literature. I. Title. II. Series.
   F204.W5M28 2005
   975.3--dc22

                                        2005012239

Table of Contents

Our Nation's House

THE WHITE HOUSE is many things. It is an office building, a private residence, a museum, a national treasure, a popular tourist site, and a symbol of the United States. For more than 200 years, this grand building has served both as a home to American presidents and as the center of the nation's political life.

Today's White House is not the same one that was built during the last decade of the 1700s. The structure had to be completely rebuilt after British soldiers burned it to the ground during the War of 1812. Since then, the White House has been renovated many times. Parts of it have been rebuilt, new rooms have been added, and others eliminated. Some changes were made to make the president and his family more comfortable. For example, in 1902 President Theodore Roosevelt was so displeased by the closeness of his

For more than 200 years, the White House has served as one of the most important symbols of the United States.

The White House plays host to several events, including the annual Easter Egg Roll, which is held every spring on the White House lawn.

family's living quarters to the offices that he demanded half a million dollars from Congress to enlarge the private areas of the home. Many times, changes were necessary to keep the building safe and stable. Over the years, steel beams have been added to support the existing foundation, and new walls and floors have replaced decayed or damaged ones.

In many instances, additions and renovations were made without much thought being given to how they would affect the building's foundation. These careless alterations led to a lot of discomfort and even danger for the president, his family, and his staff. In 1949 President Harry Truman and his family were forced to leave the White House because it was at risk of collapsing around them.

Today, the White House is administered by the National Park Service, which ensures that both the house and the grounds are safe, attractive, and functional. The building is recognized around the world and is visited by more than a million tourists every year. From its beginnings as a home for the president to its position as a symbol of the United States, the White House has had a long and often surprising history.

Planning the White House

WHEN GEORGE WASHINGTON was elected the first president of the United States in 1789, there was no home set aside for the president's use. The nation's capital was New York City, and Washington, his wife, Martha, and their family lived in several rented houses there during 1789 and 1790. When the capital moved to Philadelphia in 1791, the Washingtons moved into a mansion owned by a friend.

The Site of the Capital

Although Philadelphia was an important city, Washington felt it was not the best choice for the nation's capital. He and many others thought that the capital should be centrally located to allow easier access from all parts of the new nation. After much debate, the states of Maryland and Virginia each agreed to donate

George Washington and his wife, Martha, relax in the living room of their Philadelphia home.

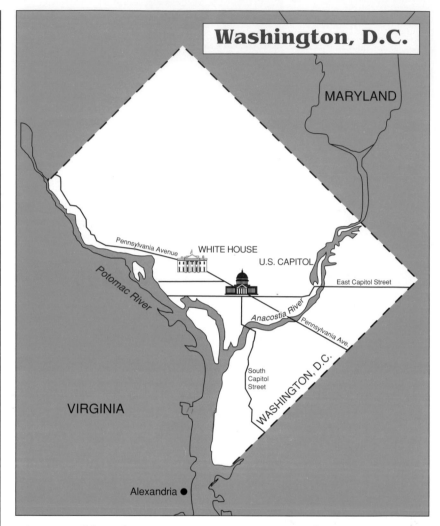

Washington, D.C.

MARYLAND

Pennsylvania Avenue

WHITE HOUSE

U.S. CAPITOL

Potomac River

East Capitol Street

Anacostia River

Pennsylvania Ave.

South
Capitol
Street

WASHINGTON, D.C.

VIRGINIA

Alexandria ●

pieces of land to create a new capital city. Because these states were on the dividing line between the northern and southern parts of the United States, the donated land provided the central location that Washington wanted.

In the summer of 1790, Washington signed a bill naming the area the District of Columbia and designating it as the nation's capital. The District of Columbia was named after explorer Christopher

Columbus. The new capital city would be called
Washington after George Washington himself.

L'Enfant's Palace

Washington asked Major Pierre Charles L'Enfant to
design Washington, D.C. L'Enfant was a French engineer and aristocrat who had served on Washington's
staff during the Revolutionary War. Part of L'Enfant's
job was to choose a site for the president's house and
to design the new home.

Washington wanted his new house to be large and
elegant, but not extravagant. Most Americans agreed
with him. They had just freed themselves from the
rule of a British king and certainly did not want their
new leader to live like a king himself. Washington was
therefore not pleased when L'Enfant came up with an
elaborate structure more suited to an emperor than a
president. Not only did Washington dislike the design,
but it was much too expensive for the young nation.
L'Enfant refused to listen to the president, however,
and insisted on his palace design. Finally, Washington
fired L'Enfant.

A Design Competition

Firing L'Enfant meant that Washington had to find a
new architect for his house. Secretary of State Thomas
Jefferson suggested that Washington hold a competition
for the design of what was being called the President's
House. Washington liked this idea, and on March 14,
1792, a gold medal or $500 was offered as a prize to "a
person who before the fifteenth day of July next shall

James Hoban

James Hoban was born in Ireland in 1762. Although his family was large and very poor, he managed to study architecture and art in Dublin. Hoban worked as a craftsman on several important buildings in Dublin, including the Royal Exchange and the Custom House.

In 1785 Hoban moved to the United States, hoping to make a good living as an architect. At first he settled in Philadelphia, but soon relocated to Charleston, South Carolina. He designed South Carolina's state capitol in Columbia in 1791.

When Hoban heard about the competition to design the President's House, he was eager to enter. He spent weeks studying drawings of stately homes before drafting his plans and sending them in. On July 17, 1792, his design won the contest.

Designing the President's House made Hoban's career. He worked for the federal government for the next thirty-nine years. After supervising the construction of the President's House, Hobart worked on the nation's Capitol, and also oversaw the rebuilding of the White House after the devastating fire of 1814. In addition, Hoban designed and built several hotels in Washington, as well as the State and War Offices.

Hoban married in 1799 and had ten children. He was a wealthy, well-known, and well-respected citizen of Washington, D.C. He died on December 8, 1831.

produce . . . the most approved plan . . . for a President's house to be erected in this city."[1] Washington himself would be the final judge.

Nine people entered the competition. One entry was signed with the name "Abraham Laws," but it was actually submitted by Jefferson. This design featured an elegant building with a large domed top. However, much to Jefferson's annoyance, Washington did not choose it as the winner.

Instead, Washington quickly settled on a design by a young South Carolina architect named James Hoban. Hoban's drawings showed a three-story house made of sandstone with a columned portico, or porch, in the front and large wings on the side. Sandstone was chosen because it would last longer than brick or wood. The design was one-third the size of L'Enfant's elaborate palace, and contained many elements of the classical style Washington admired. Classical architecture mimicked the buildings of ancient Greece and featured large, open spaces and many tall columns. Washington also liked the unusual details Hoban included, such as an oval reception room on the south side of the building.

Construction Begins

Although Washington chose Hoban's design, he did make some changes to simplify the plan. Hoban's design called for more than 100 rooms on three floors. Washington thought this was too big, so he eliminated the third floor. Washington also decided to leave out the front portico and the large side wings. Despite these changes, though, the house would still be the largest and most luxurious home in the United States.

Washington's changes reflected his concerns not only with how much the building would cost, but also with obtaining the required materials. At the time, stone was being used to construct the Capitol, the building where Congress would work. Washington worried that there would not be enough high-quality sandstone to complete both the Capitol and a large residence.

Hoban agreed to Washington's changes and was chosen as the principal architect overseeing the project. There was a great deal of work to be done before construction could begin. The president's new home would be located on a swampy patch of ground overlooking the Potomac River. Between March and October 1792, slaves from nearby plantations in Virginia cleared the land of brush and trees while workmen began digging the home's foundation. Still more workers went to a government sandstone quarry in Aquia, Virginia, to get the stone needed to construct the building.

Slave and Free Labor

By early fall, the President's House was well under way. Slaves did much of the backbreaking work. Some groups of slaves used shovels to dig the foundation, while others traveled by wagon to the quarry to cut the rough stones. Master stonemason Collen Williamson trained the slaves at the quarry. The slaves then transported the cut stones to the building site, where they were prepared and put into place by skilled Scottish workmen. The site's remote location, far from any established cities or towns, made it difficult and costly to transport the materials. Everything had to be moved on large carts pulled by horses, which was a slow and tedious process.

Both slaves and free African Americans worked at the building site along with white workmen, cutting

wood and making bricks to line the stone walls. They made bricks by mixing clay and water, shaping this mixture into rectangular blocks, and then baking the blocks in a kiln. The bricks were stacked and stuck together with mortar.

Between May and October, the laborers often worked seven days a week in brutally hot, humid weather. They had to contend with insect-borne diseases such as malaria and yellow fever, extreme heat, and heavy rain. Workers also faced primitive and unsanitary conditions. There were no toilets or running water, so the men had to use outdoor ditches called latrines. Often waste material found its way into the water supply, making the water unhealthy to drink.

George Washington (left, center) and James Hoban discuss the construction of the first White House in this 1798 painting.

The Cornerstone

Despite the obstacles, work progressed, and on October 13, 1792, the cornerstone of the house was laid. The ceremony included an elaborate procession of city officials, craftsmen, laborers, and the general public. After officials made speeches, a brass plate was set in the mortar of the foundation stone. The plate read in part: "This first stone of the President's House was laid the 13th day of October 1792, and in the seventeenth year of the independence of the United States of America."[2]

Problems and Progress

Although the building was well under way, Hoban was frustrated by a constant lack of money. Because the United States was a young nation, its treasury was too small to support such a large building project, and government officials were cautious with the nation's

Pictured here is how the White House looked in the early nineteenth century.

finances. Hoban could not get the funds to pay his workers or buy materials without getting permission from Congress. This process took so long that part of the house rotted and had to be replaced before the building could be finished.

Hoban estimated that it would take eight years to complete the President's House. Consequently, Washington did not plan to move the government to the new city until 1800. Meanwhile, work went on. Much of the building, including the floors, fireplace mantels, and doors, was constructed by hand. The need to build everything from scratch added to the duration and expense of the project.

The Final Design

Finally, in 1800, the President's House was nearly completed. The final building measured 168 feet (51.21m) across and 85 feet (25.91m) from front to back. It had two floors. The first floor contained seven rooms for official and public use. These rooms included the East Room, which could hold large numbers of guests, and the State Dining Room, where formal dinners would be held. Twenty-nine more rooms were located in the basement and on the second floor. The second-floor rooms featured family living quarters and office space, while the basement included the servants' quarters, the kitchen, and several storage rooms. The construction had cost $232,372 (more than $5.6 million today). John and Abigail Adams would be the first family to move into the house and officially make the residence the President's House.

Improvements— and Disaster

ALTHOUGH GEORGE WASHINGTON called for the President's House and helped design it, he left office in 1797 and died two years later, before the building was completed. Instead, John Adams, the second president of the United States, was the first to move into the house. He was determined to live there, even though work on the building had stopped in 1799 because laborers and money were shifted to completing the Capitol instead. Although the building was not quite finished, it was considered livable, so the Adams family prepared to move.

Blessings and Complaints

On November 1, 1800, Adams moved into the stately home on the banks of the Potomac River. That night, he wrote a letter to his wife, Abigail. In it, he said, "I pray Heaven to bestow the best of blessings on this house and all that shall hereafter inhabit it. May none

In this illustration, First Lady Dolley Madison rescues a portrait of George Washington before British troops set fire to the White House in 1814.

but honest and wise men ever rule under this roof."[3] These words are now engraved on the fireplace mantel in the State Dining Room.

Adams moved into a building with many problems. The rooms were damp because of the surrounding swampy areas, cold winds swept in through windows that as yet had no glass, and there was a huge hole in the floor where the Grand Staircase would be. When Abigail joined her husband two weeks later, she was shocked by the conditions in her new home. Some of the plaster on the walls was still wet, and some of the rooms were not plastered at all. Most of the rooms were empty, and there was hardly any furniture. So much work still needed to be done that only six rooms could be used.

For the next four months, as work slowly progressed on the house, Adams had to put up with workmen stomping through the house and tracking mud over the floors. She also struggled to find enough wood to fuel the thirteen fireplaces and keep the house warm. More confusion was added by the crowds of visitors who swarmed through the house every day, eager to see their president's home and take advantage of the fact that no invitations were needed to enter the building. Things became so chaotic that visitors were finally required to get a written pass before they could enter the house.

The difficult living conditions were made worse by the lack of modern conveniences. Like most buildings of the day, the President's House had no indoor plumbing. Water was brought in from wells, and residents had to use chamber pots or go outside to the outhouse when they had to go to the bathroom. The house also had no closets.

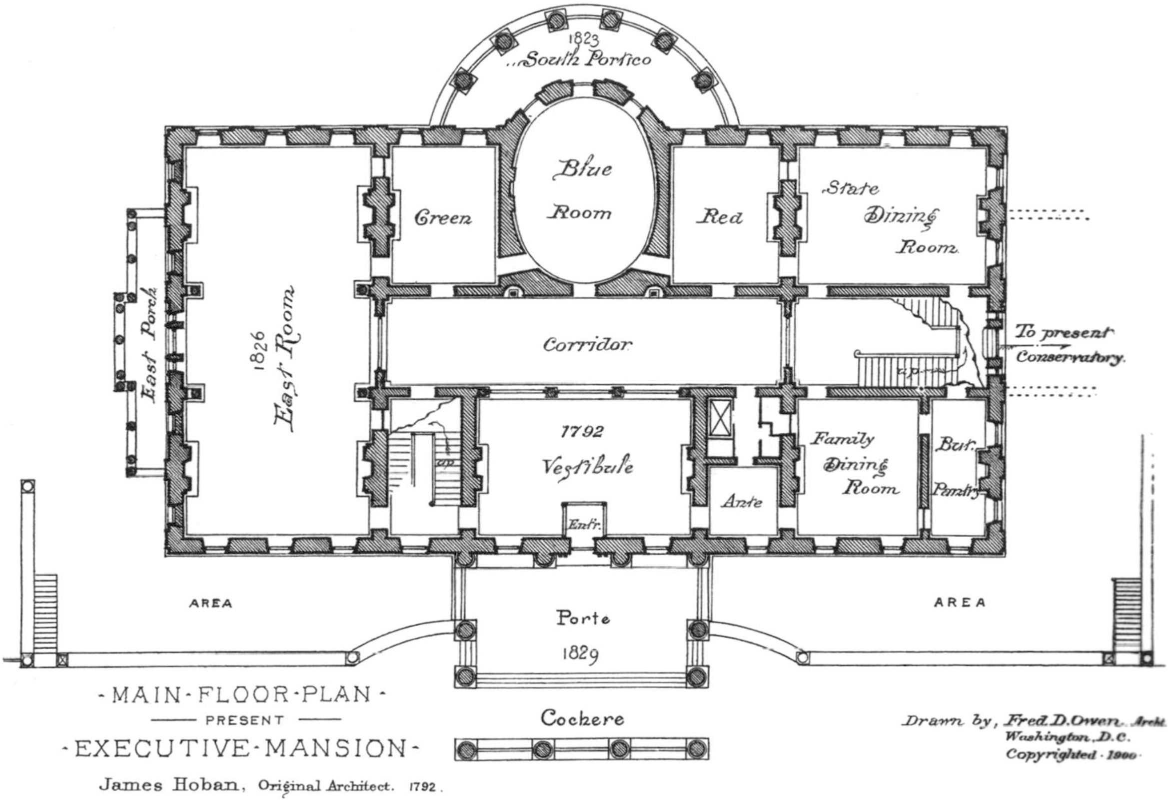
1823
South Portico
Blue Room
Green
Red
State Dining Room
East Porch
1826 East Room
Corridor
To present Conservatory.
1792 Vestibule
Entr.
Ante
Family Dining Room
But. Pantry
AREA
AREA
Porte 1829
Cochere
·MAIN·FLOOR·PLAN·
PRESENT
·EXECUTIVE·MANSION·
James Hoban, Original Architect. 1792.
Drawn by, Fred. D. Owen. Archt. Washington, D.C. Copyrighted · 1900 ·

This floor plan of the White House from 1900 shows James Hoban's original design together with additions made in later years.

The exterior of the house was in no better condition than the interior. Workmen's tools were scattered against the outside walls, trash littered the house and grounds, and the muddy landscape was crowded with sheds where the workmen lived or stored supplies. In a letter to her sister, Adams complained, "We have not the least fence, yard, or other conveniences without, and the great unfinished audience room [the East Room] I make a drying-room of, to hang clothes in."[4] However, even during the most difficult times, Adams could see that the house, now nicknamed the White House because of its whitewashed exterior walls, would one day be a splendid home.

Jefferson's Improvements

John and Abigail Adams lived in the house for only four months before his term as president ended. The next resident was Thomas Jefferson. Jefferson enjoyed entertaining and was determined to make his home more livable and elegant. He hired Benjamin Henry Latrobe, the architect of the Capitol building, to do the work. Latrobe was not impressed by James Hoban's design or construction. He often complained that the work had been poorly done.

Latrobe's first assignment was to replace the slate roof, which not only leaked, but was so heavy that it was cracking the walls of the house. Latrobe designed a lighter but stronger roof made of sheet iron. He wanted to make many other improvements under Jefferson's direction, but like Hoban before him, he had trouble getting funding from Congress because any available construction money was going toward the completion of the Capitol. Latrobe did manage to complete a driveway at the north front of the building. He also constructed two wings that included an icehouse, smokehouse, wine cellar, servants' quarters, stables, and other rooms.

Jefferson took other measures to improve the appearance of the grounds, such as having the trash and materials cleaned from the site. He arranged for the south lawns to be for the president's private use and the north lawns for public use, and also had grassy mounds built on the south lawns to make them more private.

Disaster

Like Jefferson before them, the fourth president and his wife, James and Dolley Madison, loved to entertain. They held many lavish dinner parties and receptions at the White House. Dolley Madison was a popular hostess with a keen sense of style. After Congress gave her money to buy more furniture, she filled many of the rooms with elegant pieces.

However, the Madisons' efforts to improve the house were doomed. In 1812 the United States and England went to war again. By August 1814, the British army was marching toward Washington, D.C. James Madison had gone to meet with the troops, leaving his wife and some servants alone at the White House.

As the British neared the city and the air filled with the sounds of their cannons, Madison knew that she would have to evacuate. She filled her trunks with important government papers and sent them to safety. Finally, on August 24, 1814, she took down a large painting of George Washington, breaking the frame to free it from the wall. Then she rolled up the painting and gave it to some friends to carry away before she and the servants fled.

When the British arrived, the President's House was abandoned. They piled the furniture and anything else they could find into the middle of each room and set the piles on fire, then threw torches through the windows to create an even bigger blaze. One eyewitness reported that the building caught fire immediately and the entire structure was wreathed in flames and smoke. Although a thunderstorm put out the fire during the night, the building was nothing but a smoky, hollow ruin by morning. Dolley Madison had managed to save several national treasures, but the building itself seemed beyond repair.

Rebuilding

THE WAR OF 1812 was over by 1815. James Madison wanted to move quickly to rebuild the White House. However, there was great debate over exactly what to build and where to build it. Several members of Congress wanted to start over and build a new house at a different location, or even in a different city. Madison, however, believed that rebuilding on the same spot would show the American people and the world that the British had not been a serious threat to Washington, D.C. He argued that if the White House was rebuilt to look exactly as it had before the war, it would become a symbol of the U.S. determination and strength in the face of adversity. Congress eventually agreed, and Madison set about reconstructing his home.

Hoban Returns

The first step was for engineers to examine what was left of the building. They discovered that the interior,

The Blue Room of the White House has been restored to look as it did during the presidency of James Monroe (1817–1825).

including all the walls and floors, had been completely destroyed, and only the basement was still standing. However, parts of the exterior stone walls remained in good enough condition to be saved and new material built around them.

Madison was so determined to restore the house to its original condition that he hired Hoban to oversee the project. Between 1815 and 1817, Hoban and his workers completed most of the work of rebuilding the White House. To make the renovation as close to the original building as possible, the new walls were made of sandstone from the quarry in Aquia, Virginia, just as the originals had been.

Although it had taken eight years to build the White House initially, rebuilding it took only three years. Time was saved because Hoban was able to use ready-made materials, such as flooring and mantels for the fireplaces. A new invention called the steamboat also allowed Hoban to move materials to the site much more quickly. Now he could float building materials to the site on boats rather than send them overland by horse-drawn carts.

More Changes

The renovations were completed in 1817, and on January 1, 1818, President James Monroe moved into the restored White House. He and his wife invited the public to tour the rebuilt mansion, and crowds of people filled the rooms. The building was not really finished, however. The plaster was still wet, the inside woodwork had not been painted, and there were no

The White House Grounds

The grounds around the White House are peaceful places filled with vast stretches of lawn and colorful flowers and trees. These fenced-in grounds are called the President's Park. The park extends from South Executive Avenue to Pennsylvania Avenue. Inside are fountains, paths, and a tennis court. Trees and flowers from every state in the nation are planted inside the park.

John Quincy Adams loved to garden and planted many different trees and shrubs on the White House grounds. Whenever he went on a trip, he brought back seeds to plant. His additions include tulips and an elm tree that still stands on the South Lawn. Another longtime plant is a magnolia tree next to the South Portico. It was planted by Andrew Jackson in memory of his wife.

The first garden at the White House was planted for John Adams in 1800. Over the years, presidents and their families have added their favorite flowers and shrubs. In 1913 Woodrow Wilson's wife planted roses, and after that the garden was called the Rose Garden.

The garden measures 125 feet by 90 feet (38.1m by 27.43m) and is located next to the West Wing. The president sometimes conducts official ceremonies in the Rose Garden. The garden was also the site of a wedding in 1971, when Richard Nixon's daughter Tricia was married there.

There are also two private gardens at the White House. The first is the Children's Garden, which was created by Lyndon and Lady Bird Johnson during the 1960s. The names, handprints, and footprints of all the presidents' grandchildren since Johnson are engraved in the flagstones. The garden also includes a lily pond. The second private garden was planted during Ronald Reagan's presidency in the 1980s. It is located just outside the Oval Office and provides a peaceful retreat for the president.

The South Lawn is the site of an annual White House tradition. Every year on the Monday after Easter, an Easter Egg Roll is held on the lawn for local children. This is a special way for the president to share his home with the public.

rugs on the floors. Monroe, however, wasted no time in ordering new furniture and decorations, paid for with $50,000 from Congress. Over the next two years, the interior work was finally completed.

The next 50 years brought a number of changes to the White House. In 1824 a porch was added to the south side of the house and became known as the South Portico. It was joined by the North Portico in 1830. Other improvements introduced modern technology. Indoor plumbing was installed in 1833. Gaslights were installed in 1848 to replace the candles

This photograph shows the South Portico, or porch, of the White House, added in 1824.

and oil lamps that had previously lit up the house. During the 1850s, Millard Fillmore installed central heating, which made the chilly mansion much more comfortable.

Fillmore also ordered the first stove to be installed in the White House. Until then, all the cooking had been done over open fireplaces. Fillmore ran into some resistance from the servants about the stove. When the cooks could not figure out how to work it, he went down to the kitchen himself to demonstrate. In 1877, Rutherford B. Hayes installed telephones. The house was wired for electricity by Benjamin Harrison in 1891.

Both residents and guests at the White House had long complained about the unhealthy and unsanitary conditions. One of the biggest problems was a canal that ran near the house. It was filled with dirty water, often had garbage and dead animals floating in it, was a breeding ground for disease-carrying mosquitoes, and smelled horrible. Finally, in 1872, the canal was filled and paved over to create a street called Constitution Avenue.

Problems Persist

Despite the many improvements, the White House was still an uncomfortable and even unsafe place to live. Some of the modern conveniences were not installed correctly. Electrical cables, improperly insulated, were tacked onto the ceilings rather than being run inside the walls. This created a constant danger of fire.

The White House's location in a swamp also created problems. The ground was so damp that the basement and the kitchens flooded during heavy rains, causing the kitchen's wooden floors to rot. When that happened, another wooden floor was simply installed on top of the decayed one. This went on for years, until there were five layers of damp, smelly, rotten wood in the kitchen. Finally, Benjamin Harrison's wife, Caroline, had enough. She ordered all the wood torn up and new floors installed.

Big Changes

The many changes that occurred during the second half of the 19th century did not satisfy Theodore Roosevelt, who became president in 1901 when the previous president, William McKinley, was assassinated. Roosevelt did not like the White House. He felt the building was so drafty and smelly that it was a "peril to health and even to life itself."[5]

Roosevelt also found the cramped quarters much too small for his large family, which included six children and many pets. The family's living quarters consisted of only eight rooms on the second floor, and they had to share the floor with offices for the president and his staff. Roosevelt complained that the situation made him feel like a shopkeeper living over his store. He soon proposed substantial changes to make the White House bigger, safer, and a better place to live.

In 1902 Congress approved Roosevelt's request for a major renovation of the White House and gave him more than $500,000 to pay for it. Roosevelt hired New

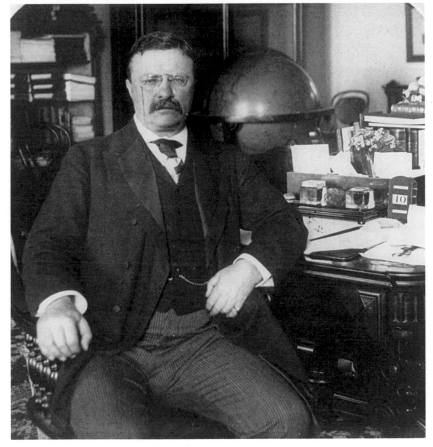

Soon after Theodore Roosevelt became president in 1901, he asked Congress to fund a major renovation of the White House.

York architect Charles F. McKim to design and supervise the renovation. Then Roosevelt and his family moved back to their home in New York City while the architect and the construction crews went to work. Roosevelt's goal was to preserve the design of the original building while making the house more suited to modern living. He told the architects to "discover the design and intention of the original builders and make it comfortable by modern standards. . . . It is a good thing to preserve such buildings as historic monuments which keep alive our sense of continuity with the nation's past."[6]

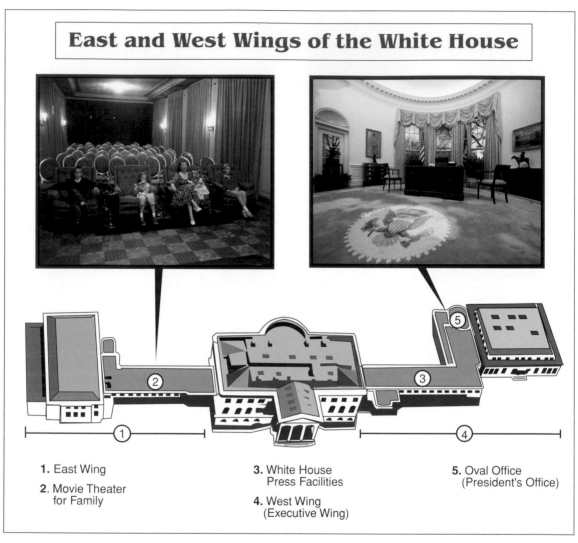

East and West Wings of the White House

1. East Wing
2. Movie Theater for Family
3. White House Press Facilities
4. West Wing (Executive Wing)
5. Oval Office (President's Office)

One of the biggest changes McKim designed was an addition to the original building, called the West Wing, to house offices for the president's staff. To make room for the West Wing, several large greenhouses next to the home were removed at Roosevelt's order to "Smash the glass houses!"[7] Moving the offices to the new West Wing allowed McKim to create more bedrooms and living space on the second floor.

Besides adding rooms, McKim also replaced the building's plumbing and electrical wiring in order to meet modern standards. The first floor was reinforced by steel beams, and an elevator was added. The interior of the house was also extensively redecorated.

Roosevelt demanded that the construction be completed in just five months. The time pressure meant that work was rushed and often sloppy. For example, instead of cleaning out sawdust and bits of wood, workmen simply left them between the old timbers of the second floor and installed new flooring over them, creating a fire hazard.

A New Name

Despite the sloppy, rushed workmanship, Roosevelt was pleased with the renovation when he moved back into the White House in October 1902. Besides the renovation, Roosevelt made another contribution to White House history. By having "The White House" imprinted on his stationery, he turned the building's nickname into its official name.

Starting Over

ROOSEVELT'S RENOVATIONS IMPROVED the White House, but the building still had many problems. It was not long before personal taste and questions of safety led to more structural changes.

New Additions

In 1923 Calvin Coolidge became president. Engineers told him that the roof of the White House was in such bad shape it might cave in. The attic floor was also falling down under the weight of the many items in storage there. In 1927 Coolidge ordered the attic and roof rebuilt with steel. He transformed the attic into a third floor to create bedrooms for staff and guests, as well as more room for storage. He also added a glass-enclosed sunroom, which he called the "Sky Parlor." The Sky Parlor was located on the roof of the South

This photograph shows visitors waiting outside the White House to visit with President Calvin Coolidge during a public reception on January 1, 1927.

Portico and was a favorite spot for First Lady Grace Coolidge.

Although Coolidge's renovations prevented the roof and attic from collapsing, the extra weight of the third floor actually damaged the White House even more. Although metal trusses were added to support the new floor, the entire weight of all the added structures was supported only by the old wooden beams on the second floor.

Fire

Construction projects, combined with sloppy wiring and debris left behind by workmen, had long created a real danger of fire at the White House. On December 24, 1929, this threat became a reality when a fire broke out in the offices, destroying the West Wing and the Executive Office Building, including the president's Oval Office (formerly the oval reception room). President Herbert Hoover watched his offices burn down, although his staff was able to save important papers from the fire. By April 1930, however, the damaged areas had been rebuilt.

Dangerous Incidents

Improvements to the White House continued during the 1930s and 1940s. In 1935 the kitchen was modernized and new equipment and plumbing were installed. In 1941 Franklin D. Roosevelt decided he and his staff needed more office space, so the East Wing was built on the east side of the house.

Recreation at the White House

The White House is not only a government building and a historical site. It is also the private home of the president and his family. Like all families, the First Family likes to have fun, and entertainment is especially important in a job that is often very stressful. For this reason, the White House includes some unusual recreational facilities that are not part of most people's homes.

Franklin Roosevelt was unable to walk because of a disease called polio. He found swimming to be relaxing and good therapy, so he had an indoor pool built at the White House in 1933. The $40,000 cost was paid for by public donations. During the 1970s, Richard Nixon had the pool filled in to create a pressroom. In 1975 workers built an outdoor pool for the next president, Gerald Ford.

Nixon's favorite sport was bowling, so he had a single-lane bowling alley installed under the driveway near the North Portico. Nixon loved bowling so much that he sometimes played twenty games in one night.

The White House also includes tennis courts, a state-of-the-art gym, billiard tables, a movie theater, and a putting green. There is even a jogging track on the grounds. Each new president is free to request recreational facilities to match whatever sport or hobby he enjoys.

Roosevelt died suddenly in 1945, and Harry Truman became president. By the time Truman was reelected in 1948, living in the White House could be quite hazardous. All the renovations and additions made over the years had left the White House in danger of collapse. Signs of stress were everywhere. The chandelier in the East Room swayed back and forth. People constantly heard cracking sounds and felt vibrations as the weakened foundation settled and sagged.

Truman had a team of engineers come in to study the White House's condition. The engineers measured the safety factor of the building by using a formula to figure out how much weight each beam or truss could bear. The higher the number, the more weight the beam could hold. In parts of the White House, the safety factor came out to less than one. Truman wrote to his sister: "I've had the second floor where we live examined—and it is about to fall down! The engineer said that the ceiling in the State Dining Room only stayed up from force of habit!"[8]

When the leg of a piano in Truman's daughter's second-floor sitting room broke through the ceiling of the dining room below, everyone knew it was time to take action. Truman noted in his diary: "Margaret's sitting-room floor broke but didn't fall through the family dining-room ceiling. They propped it up and fixed it. Now my bathroom is about to fall into the Red Parlor. They won't let me sleep in my bedroom or use the bath."[9]

Truman submitted a request to Congress for $5.4 million to completely renovate the building. Some members of the government felt that this was too expensive. One congressman, Clarence Cannon, suggested that tearing the whole building down and starting over would save at least a million dollars. However, Truman and the American public were vehemently opposed to this idea. It was unthinkable to tear down such an important American symbol.

Truman wrote to Cannon: "My suggestion is that we do not tear down the present building. The outside walls are in good condition. . . . We could put a steel and concrete structure inside the walls and restore the inside of the house to its original condition. We are saving all the doors, mantels, mirrors, and things of that sort so that they will go back just as they were."[10] Ultimately, Congress agreed to finance an extensive restoration, and architect Lorenzo S. Winslow was hired to oversee the enormous job.

Gutted

In 1949 Truman and his wife and daughter moved out of the White House. For the next three years, they lived in Blair House, a government building located across the street. Once the Trumans moved out, the construction crews moved in.

The interior of the White House was completely gutted. All the walls, floors, and ceilings were taken out, until only the outside walls were left standing. As Truman had suggested, the interior pieces were numbered and placed in storage so that the inside could be reconstructed.

Bulldozers dug a new basement two levels deeper than the previous one to provide more storage room and space for heating and air conditioning equipment. The extra levels also allowed for a 27-foot-deep (8.23m) concrete base that supported a new 800-ton (725.75 metric ton) steel framework inside the walls. Installing the new framework created some unique challenges when workers found it was difficult to get the large new beams through the narrow windows Hoban had designed 160 years earlier.

The White House Today

Today, the main building of the White House contains four levels above ground, including bedrooms on the second floor, for the president and his family. There are also multiple basement levels below the structure. Shown here are the floor plans for the first and ground floor.

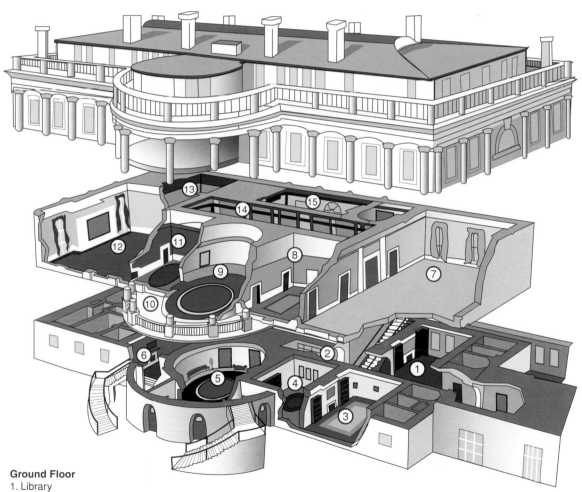

Ground Floor
1. Library
2. Ground Floor Corridor
3. Vermeil Room
4. China Room
5. Diplomatic Reception Room
6. Map Room

First Floor
7. East Room
8. Green Room
9. Blue Room
10. South Portico

11. Red Room
12. State Dining Room
13. Family Dining Room
14. Cross Hall
15. Entrance Hall

The White House grew from 62 to 100 rooms. Up-to-date electrical and mechanical systems were installed, and the whole building was fireproofed. From the outside, the White House looked as it always had. Inside, it was finally a safe place to live. In March 1952, the Trumans moved back in.

An American Treasure

In 1960 John F. Kennedy became president. His wife, Jacqueline, had a great appreciation for style, beauty, and history. She considered the White House to be an American treasure and wanted it to reflect the history of the United States. In 1961 she began acquiring furniture and artwork that had historical significance to either the White House or the nation. Some of these pieces were purchased with money from Congress, while others were donated.

In 1962 Kennedy decided to show the world the results of her work. She invited a television crew to film her as she toured the house and described its historical treasures. The special was a tremendous success, and one-third of the nation watched this personalized TV tour of the White House. President Kennedy applauded his wife's project. "After all," the president said during the show, "history is people—and particularly in great moments of our history. So when we have, as we do today, Grant's table, Lincoln's bed, Monroe's gold set, all these make these men more alive. I think it makes the White House a stronger panorama of our great story."[11]

The White House Today

The panoramic story of the White House itself continued beyond the Kennedy administration. Although the interior renovations of 1949–1952 were so substantial and well-done that very little work has been needed since then, in 1977 Jimmy Carter had the exterior of the White House renovated. More than 40 coats of paint were removed and cracks in the sandstone walls were repaired. Since then, other presidents have redecorated individual rooms or changed their purpose, but there has been no major renovation.

Today, the National Park Service is in charge of the White House and the surrounding grounds. Engineers and workers are constantly looking at ways to improve the building's efficiency and comfort and ensure it remains in good shape. The White House is truly a part of American history. It has stood as a symbol of the United States for more than 200 years, and the government plans to keep it standing forever.

Notes

Chapter 1: Planning the White House

1. Quoted in National Endowment for the Humanities EDSITEment, "How Was the White House Designed?" http://edsitement.neh.gov/view_lesson_plan.asp?id=464.

2. Quoted in Rense.com "1792—Strange Secrets of the White House." http://rense.com/general61/strrn.htm.

Chapter 2: Improvements—and Disaster

3. Quoted in The White House Historical Association, "Building the White House." www.whitehousehistory.org/04/subs/04_a02_c.html.

4. Quoted in Colonial Hall, "Colonial Hall: Biography of Abigail Smith Adams." www.colonialhall.com/adamsj/adamsAbigail.php.

Chapter 3: Rebuilding

5. Quoted in Perry Wolff, *A Tour of the White House with Mrs. John Kennedy.* Garden City, NY: Doubleday, 1962, p. 22.

6. Quoted in Wolff, *A Tour of the White House with Mrs. John Kennedy*, p. 26.

7. Quoted in The White House Historical Association, "Building the White House."

Chapter 4: Starting Over

8. Quoted in Margaret Truman Daniel, "Harry S. Truman," Project Whistlestop; Harry S. Truman Presidential Library. www.krohm.com/tewsp/ds2/ds2_4b.htm.

9. Quoted in Truman Daniel, "Harry S. Truman."

10. Quoted in The White House Historical Association, "Building the White House."

11. Quoted in Wolff, *A Tour of the White House with Mrs. John Kennedy*, p. 230.

Chronology & Glossary

1790—Maryland and Virginia donate land to create the District of Columbia and a new capital city named after George Washington.

1791—George Washington selects Pierre Charles L'Enfant to design the capital and the President's House.

1792—L'Enfant is fired. James Hoban wins a national design competition to build the President's House. The cornerstone is laid on October 13.

1799—Work on the house stops temporarily to allow workers and materials to be used for building the Capitol.

1800—John and Abigail Adams move into the unfinished house.

1801—Thomas Jefferson moves in and orders several architectural and structural improvements to the White House, including a stronger roof.

1814—On August 24, British troops burn the White House to the ground.

1815—James Hoban is hired to oversee the rebuilding of the White House.

1815–1817—The White House is rebuilt and the grounds improved.

1824—The South Portico is added.

1830—The North Portico is added.

1833—Indoor plumbing is installed.

1848—Gaslights are added.

1872—An unsanitary canal near the White House is filled and paved over to create Constitution Avenue.

1877—Telephones are installed.

1889—First Lady Caroline Harrison orders the rotting kitchen floors torn up and replaced.

1891—The White House is wired for electricity.

1902—Theodore Roosevelt receives more than half a million dollars from Congress to renovate the building. The West Wing is added.

1927—Calvin Coolidge replaces the roof, adds a third floor, turns the attic into guest rooms and storage rooms, and adds a sun-deck.

1929—Fire destroys the West Wing.

1930—The West Wing is rebuilt.

1935—The kitchen is modernized.

1941—Franklin Roosevelt oversees construction of the East Wing to provide more office space.

1948—Harry Truman complains that the White House needs major repairs and that the building is too dangerous to live in.

1949–1952—The White House is completely gutted and reconstructed.

1961—First Lady Jacqueline Kennedy begins collecting historical paintings and furnishings to redecorate the White House.

1962—Jacqueline Kennedy gives a televised tour of the White House to show off the building's historical significance.

1977—Jimmy Carter has the exterior of the White House renovated.

Glossary

classical—In the style of the ancient Greeks and Romans.

cornerstone—A stone forming part of a corner in a wall, usually laid at a formal ceremony.

kiln—A very hot oven in which bricks are baked.

portico—A porch or walkway with a roof supported by a row of columns.

renovation—The restoration and repair of a building.

trusses—Metal frameworks used to support part of a building.

whitewash—A liquid compound of lime and water used to whiten a surface.

Books

Barbara Silberdick Feinberg, *The Changing White House.* New York: Children's, 2000.

Leonard Everett Fisher, *The White House.* New York: Holiday House, 1989.

Paula Guzzetti, *The White House.* Parsippany, NJ: Dillon, 1996.

Kathleen Karr, *It Happened in the White House.* New York: Hyperion Books for Children, 2000.

Deborah Kent, *The White House.* Chicago: Children's, 1994.

Patricia Ryon Quiri, *The White House.* New York: Franklin Watts, 1996.

Steven Thomsen, *The White House: The Home of the President of the United States.* Mankato MN: Capstone, 1991.

Perry Wolff, *A Tour of the White House with Mrs. John Kennedy.* Garden City, NY: Doubleday, 1962.

Web Sites

Building the White House: The White House Historical Association (www.whitehousehistory.org/04/subs/04_a02/c.html). Featuring many photographs and other artwork, this site offers a detailed look at how the White House was built and changed.

Colonial Hall: Biography of Abigail Smith Adams. (www.colonial hall.com/adamsj/adamsAbigail.php.) This Web site features a detailed biography of Abigail Adams, the nation's first lady.

How Was the White House Designed? (http://edsitement.neh. gov/view_lesson_plan.asp?id=464). This National Endowment for the Humanities site features a description of the White House's design and a lesson plan for teaching students about it.

Project Whistlestop; Harry S. Truman Presidential Library. (www.krohm.com/tewsp/ds2/ds2_4b.htm.) Excerpts can be read from

President Harry Truman's diary describing the dangerous conditions at the White House at this Web site.

1792—Strange Secrets of the White House (http://rense.com/general 61/strrn.htm). This site describes some little-known facts about the White House and its architect.

Welcome to the American Presidency (http://ap.grolier.com/article? assetid=a2031670-h&templatename=/art.html). This online encyclopedia provides an overview of the White House's construction and renovations.

The White House: An American Treasure: White House History (http://clinton4.nara.gov/WH/glimpse/top.html). Providing an overview of the White House's history and how various presidents have changed the building inside and out, this site includes many photographs and links to related sites.

The White House: Humble Beginnings (http://architecture. about.com/library/weekly/aa011501a.htm). This look at the architecture of the White House includes floor plans and a brief history of the building.

Index

About the Author

Joanne Mattern has written more than 150 books for children, including *The Chunnel, Forensics, Homes, Transportation, The Press Secretary, The Attorney General,* and *The First Lady* for Blackbirch Press. She enjoys writing about American history, famous people, sports, and animals, and loves learning new topics as she researches her books. Ms. Mattern lives in New York State with her husband, three daughters, and assorted pets.